Healthy meals for Babies & Toddlers

Healthy meals for
Babies&
Toddlers

Valerie Barrett

This edition published in 2010
Love Food ® is an imprint of Parragon Books Ltd

Parragon
Queen Street House
4 Queen Street
Bath BA1 1HE, UK

ISBN: 978-1-4075-8117-0
Printed in China

Produced by the Bridgewater Book Company Ltd

Text: Valerie Barrett
New photography: Clive Bozzard-Hill
Home economist: Valerie Barrett
Illustrations: Anna Andrews

Notes for the Reader

This book uses imperial standard, metric, and U.S. cup measurements. Follow the same units of measurement throughout; do not mix imperial and metric. All spoon measurements are level: teaspoons are assumed to be 5 ml, and tablespoons are assumed to be 15 ml. Unless otherwise stated, milk is assumed to be whole, eggs and individual vegetables, such as potatoes, are medium, and pepper is freshly ground black pepper. Recipes using raw or very lightly cooked eggs should be avoided by infants, the elderly, pregnant women, convalescents, and anyone with a chronic condition. Whole nuts and seeds are not recommended for children under five years of age. Nut butters and finely chopped or crushed nuts and seeds are suitable for babies of one year or older, unless there has been a history of allergies to nuts or seeds within the family. If you have any concerns, please discuss it with your health practitioner. The times given are an approximate guide only.

Picture Acknowledgments

The publisher would like to thank the following for permission to reproduce copyright material: Getty: front cover image; Corbis/David Raymer: 5 middle right; Corbis/Envision: 14 right; iStockphoto/René Mansi: 7 right; iStockphoto/Elena Korenbaum: 8 left; iStockphoto/Marcelo Wain: 8 middle; iStockphoto/Karen Squires: 9 left; iStockphoto/Thomas Perkis: 9 middle; iStockphoto/Zoran Mircetic: 10; iStockphoto/Ramona Heim: 14 left; iStockphoto/Boris Yankov: 17 left; and Jupiter Images: 8 right and 16.

contents

introduction   6

first tastes   18

establishing solids   28

encouraging self-feeding   40

new tastes & textures   52

tasty adventures   66

joining family meals   80

index   96

introduction

Creating a happy and healthy home environment where a child can grow and thrive is every parent's aim. Food plays a major part in this, because good health stems from good nutrition. This book will give you information about nutrition, advice on feeding your baby from weaning to preschool, and recipes and tips that will help you make delicious everyday meals your child will enjoy.

When babies are born we always wish them good health and happiness. As a parent you can lay the foundation for a lifetime of good health by making sure they have a well-balanced, nutritious diet and that they establish good eating habits and learn to enjoy a wide range of foods. A good diet will reduce their risk of developing certain illnesses both in childhood and in adult life.

The first few years of parenthood are a roller-coaster journey of discovery and learning. No sooner have you mastered the art of breast- or bottle-feeding than it's suddenly time to introduce solids. As a first-time parent this is all new and rather scary. Armed with a little helpful information and a few good tips and recipes, however, you will find it is really straightforward. Introducing your child to new foods, tastes, and textures will help to continue the bond you have formed when breast- or bottle-feeding, and mealtimes will become opportunities for socializing and training.

As for the second wish—happiness—a healthy, well-fed child is certain to be a happy child, too. Happiness comes from feeling part of a family and being together. Mealtimes are about more than just food—they are about sharing and bonding with family members. With life today being so hectic, it is easy to slip into the habit of eating on the go or at different times, depending on everyone's needs. By sharing a meal, your baby will watch and copy you and so learn how to hold a spoon, how to eat, and how to behave. By cooking the food yourself, you will know that everything is fresh and nutritious.

making the right choices

Nutrition is a very complicated science and babies and children have very different needs from adults. You may not spend much time thinking about your own nutrition, but you certainly need to consider that of your child. This may well lead you to think more about what you eat—certainly if you have been through a pregnancy, you will have already started to do this. So the first step is to think about your own diet, because within a couple of years your child will be eating along with you.

Here are some simple steps to help a parent switch to a healthier diet:

- Eat more vegetables and fruits
- Cut down on sugary foods
- Cut down on salt by using other flavorings, such as herbs and spices
- Cut down on fat and opt for skim or lowfat milk
- Choose lean cuts of meat and reduce the amount of meat you eat by mixing it with beans
- Eat carbohydrate-rich foods, such as bread, pasta, and rice, but don't add a lot of sauces, butter, or oils to them.

CARBOHYDRATES

There are two main types of carbohydrate: complex (or starchy) carbohydrates—found in potatoes, rice, pasta, bread, and cereals—and simple (or refined) carbohydrates, such as sugar. Both types are turned into glucose in the body, which is then used for energy. Complex carbohydrates are a good source of vitamins, minerals, and fiber, and they release energy slowly over a long period of time. Refined carbohydrates provide calories but no nutrients. They are turned into glucose very rapidly, producing a short-lived energy "burst," which is followed by an energy "low." Because refined sugar is cheap and tastes good, it is added to many manufactured foods.

FAT

Fat is an essential nutrient, which protects internal organs and keeps tissue healthy. Fat contains a lot of calories in a small volume and is a very concentrated source of energy. This is good for babies, who require a lot of calories but have small stomachs. Babies and toddlers should not be given a low-fat diet. Fat is also needed to help the body absorb and use the fat-soluble vitamins A, D, E, and K.

VITAMINS AND MINERALS

Vitamins support the immune system, help the brain function, and help to convert food into energy. They are needed for healthy skin and hair, controlling growth, and balancing hormones. Vitamins are only required in small amounts and can be found in a wide variety of foods. There are two types: fat-soluble vitamins A, D, E, and K, which can be stored in the body, and water-soluble vitamin C and B group vitamins, which need to be taken daily in the diet and which are destroyed by cooking. Minerals are inorganic substances needed for a range of body functions. There are many minerals that we need, the two most important for children being calcium and iron.

PROTEINS

Proteins are made up of amino acids and are essential for the building and repair of all cells and tissues in the body. Proteins from animal foods contain all of the essential amino acids, while those from vegetables tend to be low in one or more. Most people get enough protein in their diet, but vegans and vegetarians need to eat a very varied diet to ensure they get enough protein. Children need more protein in relation to their size than adults do, so it is important to make sure they get enough.

Animal sources of protein:
● Meat
● Fish
● Poultry
● Eggs
● Dairy products

Vegetable sources of protein:
● Lentils
● Beans—cannellini beans, chickpeas, kidney beans
● Grains—wheat, rice, oats, millet, rye, and foods made from them, such as bread and pasta
● Soybeans and products, such as tofu
● Nuts
● Seeds

FIBER

High-fiber foods are too bulky and filling for babies. They are also too low in calories. Your baby will get enough natural fiber from fruits and vegetables.

weaning plan

Over the months the amount of food your baby takes will increase gradually. Don't be tempted to rush, but be guided by your baby's appetite.

	ON WAKING	BREAKFAST	LUNCH	SNACK	EVENING
STAGE 1 *(around 6 months)*	Breast- or bottle-feed	Infant rice mixed with baby's usual milk (1–2 teaspoons); breast- or bottle-feed	Breast- or bottle-feed	Breast- or bottle-feed	Breast- or bottle-feed
STAGE 2 *(around 6½ months)*	Breast- or bottle-feed	Infant rice mixed with baby's usual milk; breast- or bottle-feed	1 or 2 teaspoons puréed vegetables or fruit; breast- or bottle-feed	Breast- or bottle-feed	Breast- or bottle-feed
STAGE 3 *(around 7–8 months)*	Breast- or bottle-feed	Infant rice with puréed fruit; breast- or bottle-feed	Puréed chicken with vegetables; cooled boiled water to drink	Puréed vegetables or fruit; breast- or bottle-feed	Breast- or bottle-feed
STAGE 4 *(around 8–10 months)*	Breast- or bottle-feed	Infant rice or oatmeal or other baby breakfast cereal with milk or water and puréed fruit; breast- or bottle-feed	Puréed or mashed meat or chicken, with beans or lentils or potatoes or rice or pasta and vegetables; slices of fruit; cooled boiled water or well-diluted juice	Yogurt with chopped, puréed, or stewed fruit; slices of toast or bread sticks and savory dips; breast- or bottle-feed	Breast- or bottle-feed, if required
STAGE 5 *(around 10–12 months)*	Babies may or may not need milk on waking, but they may be thirsty, so offer water or well-diluted fruit juice.	Oatmeal or breakfast cereal with fresh fruit; slices of toast; breast- or bottle-feed	Chopped meat or chicken, with beans, lentils, rice, pasta, potatoes, or bread and vegetables; slices of fruit and/ or yogurt or milk dessert; water or well-diluted juice	Pasta dish or soup; bread or slices of toast; fresh fruit; breast- or bottle-feed	Breast- or bottle-feed, if required

Continue to offer breast- or bottle-feeds between meals if your baby wants them, but as meals become more established, you will find that your baby will need less of these. Offer small healthy snacks if your baby is incredibly active because this will keep up energy levels.

how much is a serving?

All babies and toddlers are different, so be guided by your own child's appetite. One- to two-year-olds need the same variety and number of servings as older children but may need fewer calories, so offer smaller portions. You don't have to worry if your child does not eat the suggested servings every single day; it is what the child eats over a period of two to three weeks that counts. The following is a guide to standard portion sizes for children one to three years and older, but remember this is only a guide and children's appetites vary enormously.

Foods are divided into five main groups and there is a different daily need for each. Starchy carbohydrates, such as bread, rice, pasta, cereals, grains, and potatoes, should be served six times daily. At least half of these servings should be whole grains because they are more nutritious than processed varieties.

Grains, cereals, bread, etc.:
- 1/2–1 slice bread
- 1–2 tablespoons breakfast cereal
- 1–2 tablespoons cooked rice or pasta
- 1–2 tablespoons cooked oatmeal
- 2 oz/55 g potato

Vegetables should be served three times a day. Serve a wide range of vegetables from orange fleshed, such as carrots and squash, and dark green, such as broccoli and spinach, through to starchy and leguminous varieties, such as peas and beans.

Fruits should be served twice a day. Try to give your baby a wide variety of fruits to obtain a balance of vitamins and minerals. Be careful when buying fruit juices and fruit snacks, because these products often do not contain much real fruit. Fruit yogurts often contain little fruit and a lot of sugar, so it is better to serve plain yogurt with fresh fruit.

Vegetables and fruits:
- 1/2–1 medium apple, pear, or orange
- 1–2 tablespoons grapes or berries
- 1/2–1 kiwi, plum, or apricot
- 1–2 tablespoons stewed or canned fruit
- 1/2–1 tablespoon dried fruit
- 1/2–1 small carrot
- 1–2 tablespoons peas
- 1–2 florets broccoli or cauliflower

There should be two servings daily from meat, poultry, fish, eggs, nuts, and beans. Try to choose lean cuts of meat and limit fried foods—broiling or oven cooking is preferable.

Meat, fish, eggs, etc.:
- 1–2 oz/25–55 g (1/2–1 slice) lean meat
- 1–2 oz/25–55 g poultry or fish
- 1/2–1 egg
- 1–2 tablespoons beans or lentils

Milk, yogurt, cheese, and other dairy products should be served 2–3 times a day. Children under 2 years need whole milk.

Dairy products:
- 2/3–3/4 cup milk
- 1–1 1/2 oz/25–40 g hard cheese
- 1–2 small (4 1/2 oz/125 g) containers yogurt

Many foods, such as milk, nuts, and fruit, contain fats and sugars. There is no need to add to this with cakes, cookies, candies, jam, and sodas. All these foods should be served only as occasional treats.

introducing foods into your baby's diet

FOOD	4–6 MONTHS	6 MONTHS +	8 MONTHS +	10 MONTHS +	1 YEAR +	NOTE
Vegetables	Cooked purées	Cooked purées and mashed	Cooked sticks	Cooked and raw sticks		
Fruits	Cooked purées	Cooked purées and mashed; some raw fruits, such as banana	Raw sticks			
Cow's milk and dairy	No	No, but can add cooked milk and yogurt at end of this stage	Add mild hard cheeses and other dairy products		Introduce whole milk to drink	Lowfat milk may be introduced after 2 years if your baby is healthy and has a varied diet
Meat and chicken	No	No, but can be introduced toward the end of this stage	Start with chicken and gradually introduce red meat; no variety meats until over 1 year and then only tiny amounts			
Bacon and ham	No	No	Can be introduced in small amounts only as high in salt			
Fish	No	No	No	No	A variety of fish can be served but children should not have shark, marlin, or swordfish	
Smoked fish and shellfish	No	No	No	No	In moderation and well cooked	If risk of allergy, wait until 3 or 4 years
Wheat and wheat products	No	No	In moderation and gradually; check for adverse reaction			
Eggs	No	No	Only well-cooked, yolk	Only well-cooked, yolk	Well-cooked, whole egg	

FOOD	4–6 MONTHS	6 MONTHS +	8 MONTHS +	10 MONTHS +	1 YEAR +	NOTE
Citrus	No	No	No	No	After 1 year	
Nuts, peanuts, and peanut butter	No	No	No	No	Introduce as ground nuts and monitor for reaction	If risk of allergy wait until 3 or 4 years; no whole nuts, pieces of nut, or peanut butter until 5 due to risk of choking
Sesame seeds and products	No	No	No	No	After 1 year and check for reaction	
Honey	No	No	No	No	After 1 year	
Tofu	No	No	Toward end of this stage			
Berry fruit	No	No	No	No strawberries	Introduce strawberries after 1 year	
Soft ripened cheeses	No	No	No	No	No	Introduce gradually
High-fiber foods	No	No	No	No	No	From 5 as part of a balanced diet
Tea and coffee, sodas, and other adult drinks	No	No	No	No	No	To be avoided in child's diet
Salt	No	No	No	No	No	No need to add extra salt
Sugar	No	No	No	No	To be avoided, except as part of cooking	
Artificial sweeteners, additives, etc.	No	No	No	No	No	To be avoided in child's diet

milks & drinks

Breast milk is the ideal food for babies in the first few months and indeed for the first year. Infant formula is fine up to one year. If there is evidence of allergy or intolerance to formula milk, a few babies may be prescribed soy milk. This should not be given unless prescribed, however, because it is high in glucose, which can cause tooth decay. Soy milk also contains plant hormones, phytoestrogens, which have not been fully researched in babies. Goat and sheep's milk are not suitable for children under one year.

Cow's milk should not be given before the age of one as the main milk source, because it is low in iron, although it is fine to use in cooking. A baby is born with enough iron stores for the first six months, but after that age needs iron-rich foods. By one year, a baby's diet should be varied enough to contain iron, and cow's milk can then be introduced.

Remember that milk is a food and often your baby will just be thirsty. Water is the best thing to offer, and, for babies under six months, use boiled and cooled tap water. Avoid bottled waters because these often have a high mineral and sodium content.

Sodas, flavored milk, and juice drinks are unsuitable for babies and young children, because they contain sugar. Even some "baby" drinks contain sugars and fruit acids, which are harmful to the teeth. Sugar-laden drinks tend to dull a child's appetite and this can lead to poor weight gain. Well-diluted (one part juice to ten parts water), noncitrus fruit juice can be given at mealtimes to babies under a year. Citrus juices, again well-diluted, can be given after a child's first birthday. Tea and coffee are not suitable for babies or young children because of their caffeine content.

cooking, freezing & reheating

Offering your baby homemade foods most of the time gives him or her the best start in life. Obviously, it is much cheaper to make your own baby food and you also know exactly what has gone into it and can ensure that it is free from any additives.

In order to make purées, you will need equipment for chopping and processing. A standard food processor will carry out all the tasks you need. If you don't want to go to that expense, however, a handheld blender or small mouli-légumes will do the job equally well. Handheld blenders often come with a small cutting bowl and are excellent for puréeing small quantities of food. A mouli-légumes is a food mill you turn by hand and is good for giving foods a final strain, so it is ideal for foods such as peas, beans, apricots, and prunes. A full-size blender generally blends liquids and is not as good at puréeing foods as a food processor. It will give irregular results and so will be disappointing. A strainer is useful for removing any bits of skin, seeds, and so on from purées.

In the early days of weaning, babies eat very tiny amounts, so it is less wasteful and very convenient to freeze individual portions of food. Spoon the cooled purée into sections of an ice-cube tray or mini plastic containers. Before six months it is best to sterilize these trays, but after that simply wash thoroughly in very hot water and scald with boiling water just before you use them. Freeze, and when solid pop the cubes into a plastic container and label clearly with the type of food and the date.

When you want to use them, take out one or more frozen cubes, put them in a small bowl, cover, and let thaw at room temperature for an hour or so, or for longer in the refrigerator. Always reheat thawed food very thoroughly in a saucepan or in the microwave and then let it cool to the required temperature. As your baby grows, you can increase the amount you serve by adding additional cubes.

Baby foods tend to heat quickly in the microwave, so heat in bursts of 10 seconds, stirring well to prevent hot spots from uneven heating. Make sure the food you offer the baby is not too hot. You may notice the frozen food is a little dry, so add some boiled water to keep the food from scorching. Always be very careful with infant rice. If left at room temperature for several hours, cooked rice can cause food poisoning and additional cooking or reheating will not destroy the bacteria. Make small amounts of infant rice each time you need to and refrigerate any leftovers. Use within eight hours or freeze for up to two weeks.

allergies & intolerances

Some children are more susceptible than others to a reaction triggered by certain foods. Generally, a bad reaction to a food, which leads to adverse symptoms but does not involve the immune system, is called food intolerance. This is the body's inability to digest some foods properly. A food allergy is different because it involves a fast response by the body's immune system when antibodies are released to fight off the presence of the "intruder" food.

If there is a family history of allergy, it is advisable to breastfeed for at least four months and longer if possible; weaning should not occur before six months and introduce new foods one at a time. Talk to your health practitioner if you are unable to breastfeed. When breastfeeding, monitor your diet because allergens can be passed through breast milk.

Symptoms of food intolerance:
- Skin rashes—eczema and hives
- Ear infections or asthma
- Bloating, excessive gas, or diarrhea
- Runny nose and coldlike symptoms
- Red puffy eyes and eyelids
- Nausea and vomiting

Symptoms of food allergy:
- Severe breathing problems, coughs, and wheezing
- Swelling of lips, eyes, and tongue
- Increase in vomiting
- Blistering in or around the mouth
- Skin rashes or hives
- Bloating and excessive diarrhea

Foods that can cause adverse reactions include:
- Gluten, found in wheat, rye, oats, and barley
- Eggs, especially the whites
- Sesame seeds and products, such as tahini
- Nuts, especially peanuts
- Citrus fruit, such as oranges and lemons
- Fish, especially shellfish
- Cow's milk and products made from cow's milk
- Soy
- Strawberries
- Tomatoes
- Chocolate
- Artificial additives, chemicals, preservatives, or dyes

Other foods to avoid giving your baby are salt, sugar, and honey. Honey can harbor the spores of *Clostridium botulinum*. An adult's digestive system can deal with these spores, but in a baby the spores can grow and produce life-threatening toxins.

Refer to the chart on pages 12–13 for the best age at which to introduce these foods. If you are at all worried about this, or if you have a history of food allergies, always consult your health practitioner.

vegetarian diet for babies

A vegetarian diet can be perfectly healthy for babies, but you may have to work a little harder to make sure the baby does not fall short on iron and vitamin B_{12}, because these are the nutrients most likely to be lacking in a vegetarian diet. The early stages of weaning are the same as for any other baby, but after about seven to eight months you will need to ensure that your baby is getting all the nutrients that meat would otherwise supply.

Good sources of protein:
Mix beans, such as lentils, with rice or pasta, dairy products, and eggs.

Good sources of iron:
Beans, eggs, green leafy vegetables, dried fruit, fortified baby cereals. Including vitamin C-rich foods, such as fruit, at the same time as iron-rich foods increases the body's absorption of iron.

Good sources of zinc:
Beans, whole wheat bread, egg yolks. For babies over one year with no allergies, ground nuts or nut butters are a good source of both iron and zinc.

Good sources of vitamin B_{12}:
Cheese, eggs, fortified baby cereals, textured vegetable protein.

A vegan diet—a diet that excludes dairy products and eggs as well as meat and fish—may be too bulky for young babies, so check with your doctor that the diet is nutritionally adequate and continue to bottle- or breastfeed for as long as possible.

first tastes *6–8 months*

There is no magic age or weight that will help you to decide when your baby is ready for weaning. The World Health Organization used to recommend that babies should be exclusively breastfed until the age of six months. More recent advice, however, is that infants should not be given solids before four months and that a mixed diet should be given by six months. The timing and rate of introduction of solids will nevertheless depend very much on the individual.

"During weaning, milk should be the main source of food, with solids as an extra."

Some mothers may be put under pressure to introduce solids too early. Before four to six months, babies' small intestines have large spaces between the cells to allow food molecules to pass directly into the blood. This allows large antibodies from breast milk to enter the bloodstream, but it also means that proteins from allergy-forming foods can pass through the intestines. At some point between four and six months, babies start producing their own antibodies and their kidneys become mature enough to cope with the waste products of solid food. This, therefore, is the best time to start solids.

Some of the clues that your baby may be ready for weaning include:

- The baby sits well in a high chair and the head is held up well
- Is still hungry after eight to ten feedings of breast milk or 40 oz/850 g formula a day and demands feeds more often
- Used to sleep all through the night but is now waking up
- Shows significant weight gain (baby's birth weight has doubled)
- Makes chewing motions and is losing the tendency to push food out of the mouth with the tongue
- Can move food from the front to the back of the mouth
- Seems interested in food when you are eating

Up until now your baby's food has been only milk, so the first solid you give should be a go-between food that is really a thickened milk, because the process of swallowing solids has to be mastered slowly. Remember that during weaning, milk should still be the main food, with solids as an extra. Rice cereal mixed with milk is overwhelmingly recommended as a baby's first food because it is very bland and gluten-free, and it has the right consistency.

Make sure the infant rice is just lukewarm and the consistency of thin cream. Use a shallow plastic or rubber baby spoon and put just a quarter of a teaspoon of rice cereal on the tip. Allow the baby's mouth to open and just touch the spoon to the lips. Don't force the spoon into the mouth. Some babies are more comfortable sucking from your clean finger. Try this two or three times and then wait until the next day to try again.

Never put rice cereal into a bottle with milk, because this could cause choking. For the same reason, you should always feed your baby in an upright position. Bacteria can quickly grow in uneaten cereal or purée, so don't be tempted to leave it on the side in order to try again later—throw it away and make a fresh batch the next day to offer your baby.

It's important to offer the baby solids at the same time each day. Make sure you are not rushed and your baby is not tired or too hungry. Midmorning or lunchtime is a good time, and if you offer a little milk first it will curb any hunger pangs.

Once the baby gets the hang of swallowing and begins to enjoy the infant rice, gradually thicken the consistency and offer it twice a day. Over the next few weeks slowly introduce some vegetable and fruit purées, maybe mixing them in with a little rice at first. Wait three days before you introduce any new foods to check for any allergic reaction. Remember that weaning should be a very gradual process.

Infant rice is the very best first weaning food. Once mixed with breast or formula milk, it is just like thickened milk. Root vegetables, such as carrots and turnips, are ideal weaning foods, because babies love their natural sweetness.

infant rice & first purées

HOMEMADE INFANT RICE

Prepare: 5 minutes

Cook: 20 minutes

Makes: heaping ¹/₃ cup (16 portions)

2 tbsp brown rice

²/₃ cup water

4–6 tbsp breast or formula milk,
   plus extra for mixing

CARROT PURÉE

Prepare: 3 minutes

Cook: 10 minutes

Servings: 1–6

1 medium carrot, about 3¹/₂ oz/100 g

POTATO & TURNIP PURÉE

Prepare: 5 minutes

Cook: 15–20 minutes

Servings: 1–6

2 oz/55 g potato or sweet potato

2 oz/55 g turnip

HOMEMADE INFANT RICE

Grind the rice to a very fine powder in an electric grinder. Mix with the water in a small saucepan. Bring to a boil and simmer gently for 10 minutes, stirring continuously. By this stage, the rice will have thickened considerably. Stir in 4 tablespoons breast or formula milk and continue cooking, stirring continuously, for an additional 10 minutes. Add more milk if the mixture gets too thick.

Remove from the heat and use a handheld electric blender to process the rice to a smooth, creamy purée. Cool the mixture. Just before offering it to the baby, add baby milk to thin it to the desired consistency. The temperature should be lukewarm.

CARROT PURÉE

Peel the carrot. Chop into 1/8-inch/3-mm dice. Either steam in a metal steamer basket in a small saucepan or cook in enough unsalted boiling water just to cover for about 10 minutes, or until soft. Drain, reserving the cooking liquid.

Purée using a handheld electric blender. Add 2–3 tablespoons of the hot cooking water or breast or formula milk and mix to a thin, slightly creamy consistency. Push through a fine strainer or put through a mouli-légumes, using the finest plate. Serve lukewarm.

Store in the refrigerator for 24 hours or freeze for up to 4 weeks.

POTATO & TURNIP PURÉE

Peel and dice the vegetables and put them in a small saucepan with enough unsalted water to cover. Bring to a boil, cover, and simmer for 10–15 minutes, or until very tender. Drain, reserving the cooking liquid.

To purée the vegetables, press them through a strainer or put them through a mouli-légumes, using the finest plate, and add enough cooking water or baby's usual milk to thin to a smooth, creamy consistency. Serve lukewarm.

Store for 24 hours in the refrigerator or freeze for up to 4 weeks.

Broccoli contains vitamins K (good for blood and bones), B, and C and is in the league of "superfoods." Offer this purée together with others, such as sweet potato purée, to make a tasty medley.

cauliflower & broccoli purée

Prepare: 5 minutes

Cook: 10 minutes

Servings: 1–6

3 small broccoli florets, hard stalks removed

3 small cauliflower florets, hard stalks removed

Coarsely chop the broccoli and cauliflower florets. Place in a metal steamer basket in a pan and steam the florets for 7–10 minutes, until tender. Purée with a handheld electric blender until smooth. Alternatively, press the vegetables through a strainer or put through a mouli-légumes, using the finest plate. Add baby's usual milk to thin to a smooth, creamy purée. Serve lukewarm.

Store for 24 hours in the refrigerator or freeze for up to 4 weeks.

You can use frozen peas for this purée—just add them to the saucepan for the last 3–4 minutes of cooking. For the best results, steam the vegetables in a metal steamer basket in a saucepan.

pea, bean & zucchini purée

Cut the beans into 1-inch/2.5-cm pieces and coarsely chop the zucchini. Put them in a small saucepan with the peas and cover with boiling water. Simmer for 10 minutes, or until tender. Drain, reserving the cooking liquid. Purée using a handheld electric blender. Use a little cooking water to thin and then press through a strainer to remove any stringy bits or pea skins. Serve lukewarm.

Store for 24 hours in the refrigerator or freeze for up to 4 weeks.

Prepare: 5 minutes

Cook: 10 minutes

Servings: 1–6

1 oz/25 g young, tender green beans

1 oz/25 g zucchini

¹/₄ cup fresh or frozen peas

Mixing stronger-tasting vegetables, such as spinach, with milder ones, such as potato, sweet potato, or squash, is a good way to introduce them gradually to your baby. Choose sweet ripe apples and pears, or the fruit purée may be too tart.

purées & oatmeal cereal

SQUASH & SPINACH PURÉE

Prepare: 5 minutes

Cook: 20 minutes

Servings: 1–6

3^1/$_2$ oz/100 g butternut squash, peeled and seeded

1 oz/25 g baby spinach leaves, washed

OATMEAL CEREAL

Prepare: 3 minutes

Cook: 5 minutes

Servings: 1–4

heaping ^{1}/$_4$ cup rolled oats

generous ^{3}/$_4$ cup water

APPLE & PEAR PURÉE

Prepare: 5 minutes

Cook: 10 minutes

Servings: 1–6

1 apple, peeled, cored, and diced

1 pear, peeled, cored, and diced

3 tbsp water

SQUASH & SPINACH PURÉE

Chop the butternut squash into small cubes. Put in a saucepan and add enough water to cover. Bring to a boil, then cover and simmer for 15 minutes. Add the spinach and cook for an additional 5 minutes. Drain, reserving the cooking liquid. Purée the mixture using a handheld electric blender. Add a little cooking liquid or baby's usual milk to thin. Serve lukewarm.

   Store for 24 hours in the refrigerator or freeze for up to 4 weeks.

OATMEAL CEREAL

Process the oats to a fine powder in an electric grinder. Put the water in a small saucepan and add the ground oats, mixing well. Bring to a boil, then simmer, stirring, for 3–5 minutes. Cool. Add breast or formula milk to thin. Add more milk if necessary as the cereal thickens on cooling. Serve lukewarm.

   Serve on day of making or freeze for up to 2 weeks.

APPLE & PEAR PURÉE

Put all the ingredients in a small saucepan and bring to a boil. Cover and simmer for about 7–10 minutes, or until very soft. Check regularly that the fruit has not caught on the bottom of the saucepan.

Blend with a handheld electric blender or press through a strainer. Thin if necessary with a little boiled water. Serve lukewarm.

Store for 24 hours in the refrigerator or freeze for up to 4 weeks.

Prunes can have a laxative effect, so on first offering you can mix this purée with a little oatmeal cereal. Dried fruits, such as apricots and prunes, have a natural sweetness and babies love the taste.

apricot & prune purée

Prepare: 12 hours' soaking

Cook: 10 minutes

Servings: 1–3

6 dried apricots, soaked overnight

2–3 pitted prunes, soaked overnight

2–3 tbsp water

NOTE

You may prefer to choose dried apricots that are organic and unsulfured. Sulfur dioxide is used to keep the bright orange color and can very occasionally trigger latent asthma or allergies.

Discard the soaking water and cook the apricots and prunes in boiling water to cover for about 10 minutes, or until very tender.

Drain. Press the mixture through a strainer to remove any skins. Mix with boiled water until a smooth creamy consistency is obtained. Serve lukewarm.

Store for 24 hours in the refrigerator or freeze for up to 4 weeks.

Cooked food is easier for a baby to digest, but about four weeks into weaning you can start to introduce some uncooked purées. Banana is an all-time children's favorite, but melon and avocado are also delicious.

no-cook purées

BANANA PURÉE

Peel and mash half a small ripe banana with a fork then blend briefly using a handheld electric blender. Don't strain banana as the result is not good. Mix the purée with a little breast or formula milk if desired. Serve immediately.

   Do not refrigerate or freeze.

AVOCADO PURÉE

Peel and remove the pit. Mash or purée one-quarter of the avocado. Mix with a little breast or formula milk to thin if desired. Serve immediately.

   Do not refrigerate or freeze.

MELON PURÉE

Cut a small wedge of melon, scoop out the seeds, and remove the skin. Cut the flesh into chunks and strain or purée. Serve immediately or keep in the refrigerator until required, but serve on day of making.

   Do not freeze.

Prepare: 5 minutes

Servings: 1–3

BANANA PURÉE

½ small ripe banana

AVOCADO PURÉE

¼ ripe avocado

MELON PURÉE

small wedge of melon

establishing solids *8–10 months*

Once your baby is enjoying first tastes, you can gradually start to introduce a wider range of foods and increase the number of meals a day from one to two and then three. Some babies rapidly progress from purées to chunkier foods and are ready at seven months, while others take a little longer. Once your baby is eating three meals a day, the solids can be given first and the milk second.

"Now is a good time to share meals with your baby."

The very first "lumpy" foods should contain bits no bigger than $1/8$ inch/3 mm. They should be soft enough to squash between the tongue and the roof of the mouth and swallow without chewing. Different textures, first ground and then chopped food, can be given as baby begins to chew. As with first tastes, introduce new foods one at a time with at least three days in between to make sure your baby has no allergic reaction to them.

Some babies start to put food into their mouths independently of you, and this should be encouraged because they may refuse food from the spoon and prefer to feed themselves. This is a good time to start giving a selection of bite-size finger food, so that baby can experiment with the new-found skills of picking up, biting, and chewing. Even when they don't have teeth, it's amazing how efficient their gums are. Good first finger foods to try include sticks of steamed vegetables or peeled and pitted raw fruit, lightly toasted bread, and rice cakes.

Signs that a baby is ready for finger foods are:
- Swallows food much more easily
- No longer pushes food out with the tongue
- Tries to use a spoon
- Uses the thumb and index finger to pick up food

As the baby becomes more interested in food and in feeding without your help, you need to watch out for foods that can be a choking hazard. Vegetables and fruits must be soft; any meat or poultry should be puréed or ground. Avoid raisins, popcorn, pieces of bread (unless very small), grapes, fries, and candies, and remember that whenever children are eating they should always be closely supervised.

You can start to give your baby some puréed or mashed family food, providing you make sure the food does not contain salt, too much fat, strong spices, or sugar, and is not likely to cause an allergic reaction. It is good to get your baby used to your cooking, and the social side of eating is a very important part of babies' development, so they should be allowed to join in as much as possible.

Commercial baby foods are useful to complement family and homecooked food, particularly when you are away from home or when time is short at home and your baby is very hungry. However, they should not replace freshly cooked food. If possible, choose organic baby food and make sure it does not contain added sugar, salt, artificial additives, thickeners, or fillers.

As more foods are introduced, babies will, of course, start to exert their independence and refuse both new foods and those they may have liked previously. It is sometimes difficult when you are in a rush or have spent time preparing food not to get annoyed at this stage. Forcing your baby to eat, however, will only lead to confrontation and frustration. If the baby refuses any food, just take it calmly away and offer it again another time. Don't be tempted to offer a sweet replacement because you are worried the baby is hungry. Babies will always eat when they are hungry. Our appetites vary from day to day and it's the same with babies; the only way they can communicate this to you is by refusing to eat, thus sending out the message "I'm not that hungry today." If you use food as a reward or a punishment, you are storing up trouble for later. Let mealtimes be about enjoyment and eating and nothing else.

It is handy to have some sauces on hand for mixing with any puréed or mashed meat or vegetables that may be left over from family meals. This way your baby gets used to the taste of your cooking instead of commercial baby food.

a trio of sauces

TOMATO SAUCE

Prepare: 5 minutes

Cook: 15 minutes

Makes: 1³/₄ cups

1 tbsp olive oil

¹/₂ small onion, finely chopped

14 oz/400 g canned chopped
   tomatoes in tomato juice

1 tbsp tomato paste

1 tsp dried oregano

pepper

CHEESE SAUCE

Prepare: 5 minutes

Cook: 5 minutes

Makes: 1¹/₄ cups

2 tbsp unsalted butter

1 tbsp cornstarch

1¹/₄ cups milk

3 oz/85 g cheddar cheese, grated

¹/₂ tsp Dijon mustard

VEGETABLE SAUCE

Prepare: 10 minutes

Cook: 30 minutes

Makes: 1³/₄ cups

1 tbsp vegetable oil

1 small onion, finely chopped

1 small carrot, finely chopped

¹/₂ red bell pepper, seeded and
   chopped

1 small zucchini, chopped

generous ¹/₃ cup unsalted vegetable
   stock

heaping ³/₄ cup strained tomatoes

2–3 fresh basil leaves, chopped

TOMATO SAUCE

Heat the oil in a saucepan and cook the onion gently for about 5 minutes, until soft but not brown. Add the chopped tomatoes and their juice, tomato paste, dried oregano, and a little pepper. Cook gently for 5–10 minutes, until the sauce has thickened a little. Purée to the desired consistency using a handheld electric blender. Blend to a smooth consistency for first tastes.

CHEESE SAUCE

Put the butter, cornstarch, and milk into a saucepan. Heat gently and bring to a boil, stirring continuously. When the sauce has thickened, add the cheese and mustard. Stir until the cheese has melted. Remove from the heat.

VEGETABLE SAUCE

Heat the oil in a saucepan and cook the onion and carrot for 5 minutes. Add the pepper and zucchini and cook for 1–2 minutes. Add the stock, cover, and simmer for 15 minutes. Add the strained tomatoes and basil and cook until the sauce has reduced and thickened. Purée to the desired consistency.

Rice is perfect for babies because it is comforting and easy to eat. Spring vegetables are used here, but experiment. Carrots, green beans, fava beans, red bell peppers, onions, or squashes can all be added to this risotto.

spring vegetable risotto

Prepare: 10 minutes

Cook: 40 minutes

Servings: 4–6

1 small leek, peeled and
   very finely chopped

1 small zucchini, very
   finely chopped

small handful of frozen peas

small piece of unsalted butter

1 tsp olive oil

heaping ³⁄₈ cup risotto rice

1¹⁄₂ cups hot no-salt or homemade
   vegetable or chicken stock

¹⁄₂ tsp dried oregano

2 tbsp freshly grated Parmesan
   cheese

Steam the leek and zucchini for 2 minutes, then add the peas and cook for 3 minutes. Melt the butter with the oil in a heavy-bottom skillet. Add the rice and cook, stirring, for 2–3 minutes, or until the grains are well coated in the butter and oil and are translucent.

Add the stock a ladleful at a time, waiting until it has been absorbed before adding more. Cook over medium-low heat for 20 minutes, stirring continuously. Add the oregano, Parmesan cheese, and vegetables and let simmer, stirring, for an additional 5–10 minutes, or until all the liquid has been absorbed and the rice is tender. Purée the risotto, mash it, or leave it as it is, depending on your baby's age, adding extra stock or water if it is too thick.

You can add a little cooked ground chicken or lamb to this dish if you like. Quinoa, a high-protein grain, is available in health food stores or large supermarkets, but you can replace it with long-grain rice.

quinoa with vegetables

Prepare: 10 minutes

Cook: 30 minutes

Servings: 1–3

2 tsp vegetable oil

2 tsp finely chopped onion

$^1\!/_4$ red bell pepper, seeded and finely chopped

$^1\!/_4$ orange bell pepper, seeded and finely chopped

2 oz/55 g zucchini, finely chopped

2 tbsp quinoa, rinsed

$^1\!/_2$ tsp tomato paste

$^2\!/_3$ cup unsalted vegetable stock

$^1\!/_2$ tomato, peeled and seeded, flesh chopped

$^1\!/_4$ tsp dried oregano or marjoram

Heat the oil in a saucepan. Add the onion and cook for 1–2 minutes, until soft. Add the peppers and zucchini and cook for 2–3 minutes. Stir in the quinoa, tomato paste, and stock. Bring to a boil, cover, and cook over very gentle heat for 15–20 minutes, until the quinoa grains are soft. Add the chopped tomato and herbs and cook, uncovered, for 2–3 minutes.

Purée, mash, or serve as it is. Add hot stock to thin if desired. Serve on day of making.

Freeze for up to 4 weeks.

This nurturing dish is a favorite weaning food in Italy. When your infant is older and ready for more substantial dishes, slightly larger pasta shapes can be substituted.

pastina with butternut squas

Prepare: 5 minutes

Cook: 15–20 minutes

Servings: 4–6

6 oz/175 g butternut squash, peeled, seeded, and chopped

1 cup dried baby pasta shapes or pastina

small piece of unsalted butter

1 tsp olive oil

2 tbsp freshly grated Parmesan cheese

Steam the butternut squash for about 10–15 minutes, or until tender, then purée or mash with a fork.

Meanwhile, cook the pasta in a saucepan of boiling water according to the package directions, then drain well and return to the pan. Add the butter, oil, and Parmesan cheese and stir until the pasta is coated, then combine with the butternut squash.

For older babies, you can leave the lamb mixture unprocessed so that the texture of the dish is slightly lumpy. If you prefer, you can replace the couscous with cooked long-grain rice.

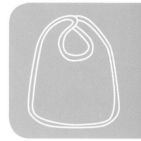

lamb with apricots

Prepare: 5 minutes

Cook: 25 minutes

Servings: 1–3

1 tsp vegetable oil

2 oz/55 g lean ground lamb

2 tsp finely chopped onion

2 oz/55 g potato, peeled and diced

2 oz/55 g carrot, diced

1–2 plumped dried apricots, chopped

$^2/_3$ cup unsalted vegetable stock

1 tsp tomato paste

2 tbsp couscous

generous $^1/_3$ cup boiling water

Heat the oil in a saucepan. Add the lamb and onion and cook for 2–3 minutes, until lightly browned. Add the potato, carrot, apricots, stock, and tomato paste. Cover and simmer very gently for 10–15 minutes. Using a food processor or handheld electric blender, blend to the desired consistency.

Put the couscous into a bowl and pour over the boiling water. Let stand for 5 minutes and then fluff up the grains with a fork. Stir the couscous into the lamb and serve lukewarm. Serve on day of making.

Freeze the lamb mixture, without the couscous, for up to 4 weeks.

You will need to mash or purée this for babies who can't cope with lumps, but by about 10 months most will manage to chew small pieces of diced chicken. Soaked, chopped prunes are also good in this recipe.

chicken with leek, mushroom & apple

Prepare: 10 minutes

Cook: 25 minutes

Servings: 1–3

2 tsp olive oil

1 oz/25 g leek, finely chopped

2 oz/55 g chicken breast, cut into
  small dice

1 oz/25 g white mushrooms,
  finely chopped

1 oz/25 g potato or sweet potato,
  peeled and chopped

1/4 small apple, peeled, cored, and
  chopped

2/3 cup unsalted chicken stock

Heat the oil in a small saucepan and gently cook the leek and chicken for 8–10 minutes, until the leek is tender and the chicken is cooked but not browned. Add the mushrooms, potato, and apple. Add the stock, cover, and simmer gently for about 15 minutes, until the vegetables are tender.

Purée, mash, or serve as it is, depending on the age of your baby.

Store for up to 24 hours in the refrigerator or freeze for up to 4 weeks.

You can vary this dish by adding cooked chopped carrot, zucchini, red bell pepper, or onion instead of, or as well as, the peas. Fresh breadcrumbs can be made using two-day-old bread and a grater or food processor.

macaroni cheese

Prepare: **5 minutes**

Cook: **25 minutes**

Servings: **1–3**

2 oz/55 g dried whole wheat
   macaroni

4 tbsp frozen peas

1/2 quantity Cheese Sauce

1 tbsp homemade fresh
   breadcrumbs

1 tbsp freshly grated Parmesan
   cheese

2 cherry tomatoes, sliced

Preheat the oven to 350°F/180°C. Cook the macaroni and peas, according to the package directions, in separate small saucepans. Drain. Mix together and put in a small baking dish. Pour over the sauce, stirring once to combine. Mix together the breadcrumbs and Parmesan and sprinkle over the top. Arrange the tomatoes on top. Bake for 10 minutes. Mash or purée as desired. Serve on day of making.

Freeze for up to 4 weeks.

Babies can dislike the texture of plums, so mixing them with apple and yogurt can make them more baby friendly. You can vary this recipe by using ripe pitted apricots with the apple instead of the plums.

apple & plum yogurt

Put the apple and plums in a saucepan with the water. Bring to a boil, then reduce the heat and let simmer, covered, for 5 minutes, or until the fruit is tender. Remove the plum skins and purée the fruit in a blender or press through a strainer until smooth in consistency.

Mix the fruit purée and yogurt together, then sprinkle over the crushed cookie, if using, before serving.

Prepare: 5 minutes

Cook: 10 minutes

Servings: 2

1 small apple, peeled, cored, and chopped

2 ripe plums, pitted

2 tbsp water

4–6 tbsp plain yogurt

1 plain cookie, crushed (optional)

encouraging self-feeding
10–12 months

As your baby reaches ten months of age, you will find that meal options increase. Babies of this age can handle new tastes and textures, and their interest in feeding themselves can be encouraged by offering a wide range of tasty finger foods and allowing them to experiment with using a spoon.

"Make sure mealtimes are calm and happy."

From around nine to ten months old, babies become more interested in feeding themselves, and will want to hold a spoon and maybe even dip it into the food and splash it around. After a lot of messy practice, they will eventually start to use the spoon as well as their fingers. Remember, the more they practice, the quicker they'll get the hang of it.

From day to day babies develop at an incredibly rapid rate. They can be very active and, although their energy and protein requirements are high in relation to their size, their appetites may be small. So as well as three meals a day plus milk, small healthy snacks—avoid those that are laden with sugar and salt—can make all the difference. Avoid giving snacks too close to mealtimes; try to space them out evenly through the day.

You can slowly start to introduce stronger flavors, but do this gradually, and watch for any allergic reaction. The term "balanced diet" can instill fear in most of us, but as long as your baby is eating a good mix of foods, including breads and cereals, lean meat, poultry, dairy products, beans, and lentils, and plenty of fruits and vegetables, then you are providing a range of nutrients.

As they eat more solids, babies need less milk. Although milk is still important, much of their calcium can now come from whole dairy products such as cheese, yogurt, milky desserts, and sauces, as well as from vegetables, such as broccoli.

If you haven't already started, now is a good time to get your baby to learn to drink from a cup. The aim is to make the change from bottle or breast to a cup by around the first birthday. This will prevent tooth decay and teeth-spacing issues. The best choice is a two-handled cup without a lid—be patient about spills. If these are a problem, then choose a lidded cup that allows the liquid to flow without the baby needing to suck. Offer water throughout the day; fruit juice should be unsweetened and diluted one part juice to ten parts water.

To ensure your baby will grow into a child who enjoys eating wholesome food, is eager to try new things, and does not become a fussy eater, make sure mealtimes are calm and happy occasions to be enjoyed. Offer food that you enjoy for the baby to sample. Don't offer mountains of food, which can be very off-putting. It is better for your baby to eat a little bit of everything than nothing at all. Make the portions small and your baby is likely to ask for more.

You may find that your baby rejects particular foods, but it's essential not to make an issue of this. Your baby is unlikely to love everything that is presented before him or her, and teething and general well-being can influence likes and dislikes on an almost daily basis.

Use brightly colored cups and bowls and always make sure you sit down at a table. Don't encourage "grazing"—eating food while moving around. Not only does it encourage bad habits, but there is always the danger of choking. Encourage mealtimes with friends. Allow plenty of time but also don't leave a child to sit too long with food if they really are not hungry. Let them go, and you will find they will make up for it at the next meal.

Keep a careful eye on babies when they start to feed themselves, because they sometimes forget to swallow and are inclined to store food in their cheeks. Make food fun by choosing different colors and textures.

bread sticks with dips

NO-SALT BREAD STICKS

Prepare: 15 minutes

Cook: 10 minutes

Makes: about 60 small
   bread sticks

¾ cup white bread flour

¾ cup whole wheat bread flour

¼-oz/7-g sachet active dry yeast
   (about 1 level tsp)

1 tbsp olive oil

about ¾ cup lukewarm water (mix
   one-third boiling water with
   two-thirds cold)

NO-SALT BREAD STICKS

Preheat the oven to 425°F/220°C. Put the flours and yeast into a bowl and add the olive oil and enough water to mix to a soft but not sticky dough. Knead for about 5 minutes, until smooth and elastic. Divide the dough into 4 pieces. Roll each piece out to a long, very thin sausage and cut into small sticks about 3 inches/ 7 cm long. Place on a nonstick baking sheet and cook for about 7–10 minutes, until golden and crisp. Serve with the dips.

Store for up to 2 weeks in an airtight container.

HUMMUS

It's worth making your own hummus for baby because prepared versions can be salty and contain tahini, a sesame seed-based paste, which can very occasionally cause an allergic reaction and is best given when your child is older. Put all the ingredients into a food processor and blend until smooth. Add a little more lemon juice or yogurt to taste if desired.

Store for up to 3 days in the refrigerator.

AVOCADO DIP

Mash the avocado with a fork and mix in the lemon juice and yogurt.

Store for up to 2 days in the refrigerator.

BEET DIP

Cut the beet into very small dice and cook in a little boiling water for 12–15 minutes, until soft. Cool. Peel and coarsely grate the apple. Put the beet, apple, lemon juice, and sour cream into a bowl and process until smooth using a handheld electric blender.

Store for up to 2 days in the refrigerator.

HUMMUS

14 oz/400 g canned no-sugar, no-salt chickpeas, drained and rinsed

1 garlic clove

1 tbsp olive oil

a little freshly squeezed lemon or lime juice

1 tbsp plain yogurt

AVOCADO DIP

1/2 ripe avocado

1 tsp lemon juice

2–3 tsp plain yogurt

BEET DIP

1 small fresh beet, peeled

1/2 small apple

squeeze of lemon juice

1 tbsp sour cream or plain yogurt

These little patties are a popular Middle Eastern street food. For older children, half fill a pita bread with shredded lettuce, cucumber, tomato, and feta cheese and top with the warm falafel and a dollop of hummus.

falafel with carrot salad

Prepare: 15 minutes

Cook: 5 minutes

Makes: 8–10 falafel

14 oz/400 g canned no-sugar, no-salt chickpeas, drained and rinsed

¼ small onion

1 tsp ground coriander

1 tsp ground cumin

1 tbsp chopped fresh parsley

1 tbsp chopped fresh cilantro

2 tbsp whole wheat flour, plus extra for dusting

sunflower oil, for cooking

FOR SERVING:

1 medium carrot, coarsely grated

½ apple, peeled and coarsely grated

2 tbsp raisins, chopped

1 tsp lemon juice

1 tsp chopped fresh mint

2–3 tbsp Greek-style yogurt

strips of pita bread

Put the chickpeas, onion, spices, herbs, and flour into a food processor and blend until smooth. With lightly floured hands, shape the mixture into small patties.

Heat a little sunflower oil in a skillet and when hot, cook the falafel for 2–3 minutes on each side, turning only once during cooking. Drain the falafel on paper towels.

Mix together the carrot, apple, raisins, lemon juice, and mint. Serve the falafel with a little of this salad, a spoonful of yogurt, and 2–3 strips of pita bread.

Make these mini meatballs small enough for your baby to pick up and eat as a finger food. You can use other meats, such as lamb, chicken, or turkey. You can also serve them with a vegetable sauce and noodles or small pasta shapes.

mini meatballs & spaghetti

Prepare: 10 minutes

Cook: 5 minutes

Makes: 8–10 meatballs

2 oz/55 g lean ground beef

1 tsp finely chopped onion

2 tsp chopped fresh basil

1 tbsp homemade fresh whole
  wheat breadcrumbs

1 tsp olive oil

¼ quantity Tomato Sauce

2 oz/55 g dried spaghetti, broken
  into short lengths

finely chopped fresh parsley
  (optional)

To make the meatballs, put the ground meat, onion, basil, and breadcrumbs into a small bowl and process using a handheld electric blender. Divide and shape the mixture into even bite-size balls.

Heat the oil in a small saucepan and cook the meatballs, turning frequently, for 2–3 minutes, until lightly browned. Pour over the sauce, cover, and simmer gently for about 10 minutes.

Cook the spaghetti in a separate saucepan, according to the package directions. Drain. Serve the spaghetti topped with the meatballs and sauce. Sprinkle with parsley if liked.

This hearty, chunky soup is full of vegetables and is served with crisp cheese sticks that baby can dunk. Try cutting the cheese dough into letters or animal shapes if you have cookie cutters.

minestrone soup

Prepare: 15 minutes

Cook: 15 minutes

Servings: 2–4

1 tbsp sunflower oil

2 tbsp chopped onion

1 garlic clove, chopped

1/2 tsp Italian herb seasoning

1 oz/25 g carrot, chopped

2 tsp very finely chopped celery

1 oz/25 g potato, peeled and chopped

1 1/4 cups unsalted vegetable or chicken stock

heaping 1/3 cup strained tomatoes

1 tsp tomato paste

1 oz/25 g dried vermicelli, broken into small pieces

1 tbsp frozen peas

10 baby spinach leaves, washed

CHEESE DOUGH STICKS

Makes: 20–24 sticks

heaping 1/3 cup all-purpose flour, plus extra for dusting

heaping 1/3 cup whole wheat flour

4 tbsp unsalted butter

1/2 cup grated cheddar cheese

1 egg, beaten

To make the soup, heat the oil in a small saucepan. Add the onion and cook for a few minutes, until soft but not brown. Add the garlic, seasoning, carrot, celery, and potato and cook for 1–2 minutes. Stir in the stock, strained tomatoes, and tomato paste. Bring to a boil, add the pasta and peas, and then simmer for about 10 minutes, until the vegetables are tender. Stir in the spinach leaves, remove from the heat, and cool a little before serving.

To make the cheese dough sticks, preheat the oven to 400°F/200°C. Put the flours into a bowl. Add the butter and rub in. Stir in the cheese. Add the egg and mix to a soft dough. Roll out on a lightly floured board and cut into 3 x 1/2-inch/ 7 x 1-cm sticks. Place the sticks on a nonstick baking sheet and bake in the oven for 5–10 minutes, depending on size. Cool.

Store the cheese sticks for 2–3 days in a container or freeze for up to 4 weeks.

Leftover meat from a roast chicken is ideal for this dish. For a vegetarian version, replace the chicken with mozzarella cheese. Disguising vegetables by making them into a sauce is a good way of getting babies to enjoy different flavors.

pasta with roasted red pepper sauce

Prepare: 30 minutes
(excluding cooling time for bell
   pepper)
Cook: 20 minutes
Servings: 1–2

1 red bell pepper, halved
2 tbsp olive oil
1 small shallot, finely chopped
1 garlic clove, crushed or very finely
   chopped
½ cup mini pasta shapes
3–6 tbsp water or unsalted chicken
   or vegetable stock
1 tbsp cooked butternut squash,
   mashed or chopped
2 oz/55 g cooked chicken breast,
   chopped or ground
1 tsp finely chopped fresh parsley

Preheat the oven to 400°F/200°C. Put the bell pepper on a baking sheet and drizzle with half the oil. Roast for about 20–25 minutes, until soft and blackened. Put into a large plastic bag and seal the top. Let stand until cold. The steam created in the bag helps to separate the skin from the flesh of the pepper. Peel the pepper and remove the stalk and seeds. Purée using a food processor or handheld electric blender.

Heat the remaining oil in a small saucepan and cook the shallot and garlic gently for about 5 minutes. Meanwhile, cook the pasta in a separate saucepan, according to the package directions.

Add the red pepper purée, stock, butternut squash, and chicken to the shallot and garlic. Heat gently for about 5 minutes, adding more stock if necessary. Drain the pasta and add to the red pepper mixture. Toss well and serve sprinkled with the parsley.

If you cannot find canned corn without added salt or sugar, use cooked frozen corn instead. If your baby has only just started chewing, then chop the corn before adding it to the batter.

cheesy corn fritters

Prepare: 10 minutes

Cook: 10 minutes

Makes: 4–6 large or 8–10 small
  fritters

1 egg

generous ¾ cup milk

¾ cup all-purpose flour

½ tsp baking powder

⅓ cup canned corn kernels without
  added salt or sugar, drained

4 tbsp grated cheddar cheese

1 tsp snipped fresh chives

2 tsp sunflower oil, for pan-frying

FOR SERVING

extra corn

mini carrot sticks

Put the egg and milk into a small bowl and beat with a fork. Add the flour and baking powder and beat until smooth. Stir in the corn, cheese, and chives. Heat a little sunflower oil in a skillet and drop either teaspoonfuls or tablespoonfuls of the batter into it. Cook for 1–2 minutes on each side, until the fritters are puffed up and golden.

Drain on paper towels and serve with extra corn and mini carrot sticks.

Babies love the bright colors and sweetness of fruits and dipping it into creamy yogurt is a good way to encourage babies to feed themselves. Always give babies under two years old whole milk yogurt, never low-fat.

fruity dippers

Prepare: 5 minutes

Servings: 1–2

½ cup raspberries

2 tbsp plain or Greek-style yogurt

CHOOSE FROM FRUITS SUCH AS:

½ small banana, cut into chunks

½ apple, peeled and cut
  into long slices

½ pear, peeled and cut into
  long slices

3–4 seedless grapes, halved

1 oz/25 g mango, cut into long
  thin slices

½ peach or nectarine, cut into slices

½ kiwi, cut into sticks

To make the dip, press the raspberries through a nylon strainer to remove the seeds. Stir the raspberry purée into the yogurt and spoon into a small dish. Arrange the fruits on a plate with the dip.

new tastes & textures
12–18 months

This is the age of the toddler, a transitional stage when your baby is no longer a baby and not quite a child yet. It is often a challenging time, when little ones assert their growing independence in many ways. Food choices expand and now is a good time to get your baby used to a variety of foods with different flavors.

"Toddlers can be surprisingly open to strongly flavored foods."

For toddlers, the world is now becoming bigger and they may enter into new things with gusto, just as they may be sceptical and cautious of anything unknown. They may switch from being a child who is happy to taste anything to being a grouchy, obstinate one who refuses even foods that have previously been favorites.

It is normal for your toddler to eat more on some days than others. Lack of appetite may have a number of different underlying causes, including teething, coming down with a cold, or tiredness. Maybe they have been drinking a lot of milk and so are not hungry. Toddlers can also be very good at using food to gain attention, because refusing food usually provokes some kind of a reaction. Here are some tips to ensure mealtimes are peaceful affairs, and eating is enjoyable and fun.

Tips on enjoyable and peaceful mealtimes:

- One way to introduce new foods is to mix them in with foods you know the toddler likes. Unpopular vegetables can be hidden in soup or pasta sauces.
- Ensure your children have plenty of fresh air and exercise so they are hungry when they eat.
- Serve small portions and don't insist that your child finishes everything on the plate—a little food is better than nothing.
- Don't offer snacks too close to mealtimes.
- When possible, allow him or her to help with the shopping and preparation—a toddler can help put apples in a bag in the supermarket and then into a bowl once at home.
- Try to ensure your baby doesn't eat alone. If you or the family are busy eating, then baby will follow suit.

- Never bargain with food. If you promise a treat if the food is eaten, it only reinforces the dislike of the refused food. Make no fuss, simply remove the food and only offer something healthy, such as fruit, until the next meal or snack.
- If a food is rejected, simply remove it and try again another time. It may take two or three attempts before the new food is accepted.
- Allow toddlers to choose sometimes. Would they prefer an apple or a banana?
- Never let a child sit for overly long while you try to get him or her to eat. The food becomes cold and unappealing and your toddler will be even less likely to eat. Remember: children never starve themselves.

Up until now your baby's diet has mainly depended on breast or formula milk. From the age of one babies can be given whole cow's (or goat or sheep's) milk, about 1 1/2 cups a day, as part of a well-balanced diet. Make the changeover slowly, especially if you are breastfeeding.

One important thing about feeding a toddler, and in fact any child under the age of five, is that they don't have the same nutritional needs as older children and adults. They need more fat and calories and less fiber. The fat and calories assist in the growth of the brain and nervous system. Without enough fat and calories to burn, the body will burn protein instead and protein is needed to build muscle. To keep their blood sugar up, toddlers need to eat and drink every two to three hours. So, although we are conditioned to eat just three meals a day, what toddlers need is three small meals with the addition of healthy, nutritious snacks in between.

Some commercial cereals are great for kids, but most are very high in refined sugar, which will give a quick burst of energy and then leave them hungry. You can make this for a baby under one year old if you omit the honey.

fruity purple oatmeal

Prepare: **5 minutes**

Cook: **5 minutes**

Servings: **1**

³/₄ **cup fresh or thawed frozen summer fruits, such as raspberries, strawberries, cherries, or blackberries**

heaping ¹/₄ cup rolled oats

generous ¹/₃ cup milk

1–2 tsp honey (optional)

plain yogurt, for serving (optional)

Take half the summer fruits and process to a purée using a handheld electric blender. Put the oats and milk into a small saucepan and simmer gently for about 5 minutes, stirring from time to time. Cool a little and stir in the honey if using.

Pour into a serving bowl and stir in the fruit purée, making a swirling pattern. Coarsely chop the remaining fruit and scatter on top. Serve with plain yogurt if liked.

Instead of parsnips you can use sweet potato. It's a good idea to vary these root vegetables so babies don't get too attached to potato fries—a variety of tastes and textures should be encouraged. The extra burgers can be frozen before cooking.

mini burgers with parsnips

Preheat the oven to 400°F/200°C. Place the parsnips in a small roasting pan and drizzle over the oil and the honey. Roast in the oven for about 20 minutes, until crisp and golden brown, turning several times during cooking.

To make the burgers, mix together the breadcrumbs, herbs, ketchup, and ground meat. Shape into small patties. Cook in a nonstick skillet for about 4–5 minutes on each side.

Serve in a roll with lettuce and cherry tomatoes, with the parsnips on the side, or omit the roll and arrange on a plate for a help-yourself meal.

Prepare: 10 minutes

Cook: 15–20 minutes

Makes: 2–4 burgers, depending on size

2 baby parsnips, washed and quartered

1 tbsp olive oil

2 tsp honey

½ cup homemade fresh breadcrumbs

½ tsp Italian herb seasoning

1 tbsp organic ketchup

9 oz/250 g fresh lean ground beef or lamb

FOR SERVING

mini rolls

baby lettuce

cherry tomatoes

Most children enjoy eggs, and this omelet is filled with vegetables, which can be as varied as you like. It is very good eaten cold and makes an excellent addition to a lunch box for an older child or even an adult.

deep pan omelet

Prepare: 10 minutes

Cook: 35 minutes

Makes: 8-inch/20-cm omelet

1 tbsp sunflower oil

½ small onion, chopped

7 oz/200 g diced waxy potatoes

½ red bell pepper, seeded and
  thinly sliced

1 small zucchini, diced

2 tbsp frozen peas

1 tbsp chopped fresh parsley

3 eggs, beaten

Heat the oil in an 8-inch/20-cm omelet pan. Add the onion and cook for about 5 minutes, until soft. Add the potatoes and cook gently for about 10 minutes, until just soft. Add the pepper, zucchini, petit pois, and parsley and cook for 2–3 minutes.

Beat the eggs with 1 tablespoon cold water. Pour over the vegetables in the skillet. Cook over very low heat for 5–10 minutes, or until the mixture is beginning to set on top and is golden underneath when the edge is lifted with a spatula.

Place under a medium broiler for 1–2 minutes, until the top is set and golden brown. Cool and then cut into wedges or strips to serve.

Ideally, you should use a wok to stir-fry, but you can also get good results using a large skillet by just stirring continuously so the ingredients don't burn. Cut everything into similar-size pieces so they cook in the same time.

sweet & sour chicken stir-fry

Prepare: 10 minutes

Cook: 10 minutes

Servings: 2

2 oz/55 g medium egg noodles

1 tbsp vegetable oil

2 oz/55 g skinless, boneless chicken breast, cut into thin strips

½ small carrot, cut into matchsticks

2 baby corn, halved widthwise and lengthwise

4 sugar snap peas, cut into strips

2 oz/55 g pineapple, chopped

2 scallions, sliced

1 oz/25 g bok choy or baby spinach, coarsely torn

1 tsp pineapple juice

1 tsp light soy sauce

1 tsp rice or sherry vinegar

FOR SERVING

soy sauce (optional)

sweet chili sauce (optional)

Cook or soak the noodles according to the package directions. Heat the oil in a wok and stir-fry the chicken until lightly browned and cooked through. Add the carrot, baby corn, sugar snap peas, pineapple, and scallions and cook for 1–2 minutes. Add the bok choy, pineapple juice, soy sauce, and vinegar and stir together until the bok choy has just wilted.

Drain the noodles and serve topped with the chicken and vegetables. Add a little more soy sauce if liked; older children may like a little sweet chili sauce with this.

If preferred, you can make one square pizza base then cut it into fingers and freeze these, uncooked, for up to 4 weeks. If you haven't time to make the dough, bread muffins, bagels, and pita breads all make good pizza bases.

first pizzas

Prepare: 10 minutes, plus time for the dough to rise

Cook: 10 minutes

Makes: 4 individual pizzas

¾ cup white bread flour

¾ cup whole wheat bread flour

¼-oz/7-g sachet active dry yeast (about 1 level tsp)

1 tbsp olive oil

about ¾ cup lukewarm water (mix one-third boiling water with two-thirds cold)

light olive oil, for brushing

4 tbsp Tomato Sauce or strained tomatoes

6 cherry tomatoes, halved

4 tsp chopped fresh oregano or basil

4½ oz/125 g mild hard cheese, such as cheddar

Preheat the oven to 425°F/220°C. Put the flours and yeast into a bowl and add the olive oil and enough water to mix to a soft but not sticky dough. Knead for about 5 minutes, until smooth and elastic. Divide the dough into 4 pieces and roll out each piece into a circle about 4 inches/10 cm round. Lightly brush a baking sheet with olive oil and lay the dough circles on top. Brush each circle with a little olive oil. Let the dough rise for about 15 minutes.

Spread a little Tomato Sauce on each circle and then top with 3 halved tomatoes and a scattering of herbs and cheese. Bake in the oven for about 7–10 minutes.

ALTERNATIVE TOPPING IDEA
Mushroom and pepperoni

Spread the pizzas with Tomato Sauce and top each with a thinly sliced white mushroom, a slice of pepperoni, snipped into very small pieces, and a tablespoon of crumbled goat cheese.

This cheese-flavored Mexican dish makes a great lunch or snack. You can make a vegetarian version using grated carrot, grated zucchini, red onions, tomatoes, and corn kernels.

chicken quesadilla triangles

Prepare: 10 minutes

Cook: 10 minutes

Servings: 1–2

2 small (8-inch/20-cm) flour tortillas

1–2 tsp melted butter, for brushing

½ small cooked skinless, boneless chicken breast, finely chopped

¾ cup grated cheddar cheese (or a mixture of cheddar cheese and mozzarella cheese)

1 tomato, peeled, seeded, and diced

FOR SERVING

2 tsp sour cream, seasoned with a squeeze of lime juice and a little chopped cilantro

Avocado Dip

Preheat the oven to 400°F/200°C. Lightly brush one tortilla with a little melted butter and place, butter side down, on a baking sheet. Arrange the chicken, cheese, and tomato over the tortilla, leaving a gap around the edge. Place the second tortilla on top and brush with the remaining butter. Bake for about 10 minutes, until the cheese has melted and the top is brown. Let cool slightly then cut into triangles and serve with sour cream or Avocado Dip.

Oranges are a good source of vitamin C, and children should be encouraged to eat the fruit because it contains valuable fiber. Sometimes oranges may have a sharp taste, so a good way to introduce them is with a creamy rice dessert.

fragrant creamy rice

Prepare: 10 minutes

Cook: 25 minutes

Servings: 2–3

¹/₄ cup short-grain rice

1 ¹/₄ cups whole milk

seeds from 1 cardamom pod,
    crushed

¹/₂ tsp vanilla extract

2 tsp sugar (optional)

milk or orange juice, for thinning
    (optional)

1 large orange, peel and pith
    removed and cut into segments

1 tsp honey

few drops of orange flower water
    (optional)

Put the rice, milk, crushed cardamom seeds, vanilla extract, and sugar, if using, into a small saucepan. Bring to a boil and simmer very gently for about 20 minutes, stirring frequently. When the rice grains are very soft, remove from the heat and let cool. Thin with a little milk or orange juice if necessary.

Put the orange segments into a dish and drizzle over the honey and orange flower water. Toss gently together and serve with the creamy rice.

Vanilla ice cream is a good base for a lot of different desserts—try it with sliced pears and chocolate sauce, or try stirring in a mashed banana, fresh raspberries, or mini chocolate chips before freezing.

ice cream with strawberry sauce & star cookies

Prepare: about 45 minutes, plus
   freezing
Cook: 5 minutes
Makes: about 2¹/₂ cups

2¹/₂ cups heavy cream

1 vanilla bean, split

4 egg yolks

heaping ¹/₄ cup sugar

1¹/₄ cups strawberries

1 tbsp confectioners' sugar

STAR COOKIES

¹/₂ cup confectioners' sugar, sifted

6 tbsp unsalted butter, softened

1 egg yolk

1 cup all-purpose flour, plus extra
   for dusting

Put the cream into a saucepan. Scrape the seeds from the vanilla bean and add them to the saucepan, together with the bean. Bring to a boil, remove from the heat, and leave for about 20 minutes.

Mix together the egg yolks and superfine sugar. Pour on the cream. Return the mixture to the cleaned saucepan and cook very gently until the mixture starts to thicken, stirring continuously. Pour through a strainer into a bowl. Cover and let stand until cold.

Churn the mixture in an ice-cream maker, or pour into a bowl and freeze. When it is half frozen, remove and whisk. Return to the freezer. Repeat 4 or 5 times.

To make the sauce, put the strawberries and sugar into a bowl and purée using a handheld electric blender.

To make the star cookies, preheat the oven to 350°F/180°C. Put all the ingredients into a bowl and mix into a smooth dough. Roll out on a floured surface and cut out star shapes. Place on a nonstick baking sheet and bake for 5–10 minutes, until golden brown. Serve the ice cream with the sauce and the cookies.

tasty adventures *18–36 months*

Your toddler is now approaching the stage that is sometimes called the "terrible twos." Children are now no longer babies and often assert their independence when it comes to what they will eat, wear, or do. Don't let mealtimes become one of the battlegrounds. This period can be a roller coaster of change and you will need a little patience, but it is a phase that can also be a lot of fun.

"Involving your toddler in mealtimes can be a lot of fun."

Children of this age are socializing much more, getting out and about, and coming into contact with different foods. This can be a difficult time because the pressure from advertising, the friends they visit, and the places they go can have a big impact.

Don't fall into the trap of giving your toddler so-called "children's food." It is very easy, when time is short, to quickly cook up some burgers or nuggets or offer potato chips or cookies. This can soon become a habit, and, before you know it, your toddler will have gotten used to the taste of processed food and won't eat fresh vegetables and homemade dishes. Products that are specifically geared for children are expensive. Most of these foods have high levels of salt, sugar, fat, and artificial additives. It is not a good idea to ban these foods altogether, because this only serves to make them even more attractive. Allow them occasionally as part of a balanced meal, and that way your child will learn that there are not "bad" foods and "good" foods, but rather there should be a sensible way of eating.

Eating out is another area that can be very challenging. Most children love the novelty of eating out, but again it should be an occasional treat, because it is often difficult to find a child-friendly restaurant that offers healthy, nutritious good-quality food. Burgers and fries or pizza are fine every once in a while as a treat, and it is good to get your toddler used to eating out and learning how to behave when not at home. Rather than opt for the children's menu (which is often something coated in breadcrumbs, deep-fried, and served with fries), it's a good idea to choose something for yourself and ask for a separate plate so your toddler can share your meal.

Sugary snacks are very appealing to young children, but they should be avoided because the enamel on new teeth is vulnerable and these baby teeth will be needed to guide in the adult teeth. Bacteria that feed on the sugars we eat or drink produce dental plaque. The plaque contains an acid, which attacks the enamel, producing holes and then breaking down the dentine inside the tooth. The more sugar toddlers eat, the more likely it is their teeth will be damaged. Restrict sugary foods to mealtimes, because eating them in conjunction with other food helps to dilute the acid generated. Don't let children have juice or milk just before a nap or at bedtime after they have cleaned their teeth: the sugar attacks their teeth while they sleep. Don't be tempted to use foods or drinks that replace sugar with artificial sweeteners, because these can encourage a sweet tooth and are not a necessary part of a child's diet.

Involving your toddler in mealtimes can be a lot of fun and also a valuable learning time. Children are much more likely to eat wisely and well if they have been involved at some point in the food preparation. Here are some ideas to encourage toddlers to be curious and adventurous about eating and food.

Tips on encouraging your child to eat:
- Teach them the names and colors of fruits and vegetables when you are shopping.
- When you unpack, count how many apples or packages you have bought.
- Let them stir a mixture with a wooden spoon.
- Use a plastic cookie cutter to stamp out shapes from bread or crêpes or pie dough.
- Let them place small fruits, such as strawberries, on a dessert.

Toddlers are often too busy running around to be interested in food, so small meals and snacks may be preferred at this stage. It's also a good time to introduce new foods before your toddler becomes too picky.

stuffed mushrooms

Prepare: 5 minutes

Cook: 15 minutes

Makes: 4–5

4–5 medium cremini mushrooms

olive oil

1 tbsp fresh breadcrumbs

1 oz/25 g Gruyère cheese, finely
   grated

1 thin slice lean ham, finely
   chopped

$\frac{1}{2}$ tsp finely snipped fresh chives

small triangles of toasted whole
   wheat bread, lightly buttered,
   for serving

Preheat the oven to 375°F/190°C. Carefully wipe the mushrooms. Remove and discard the stalks and brush the outside of the mushrooms with olive oil.

Mix the breadcrumbs, cheese, ham, and chives together and pack the mixture into the mushrooms.

Place on a baking sheet and bake for 10–15 minutes, until golden brown. Serve with triangles of buttered whole wheat toast.

A great way to get kids to eat vegetables is to "hide" them in something tasty, such as pasta and tomato sauce. In this recipe, onions, zucchini, and baby spinach are all included in the delicious children's favorite, lasagne.

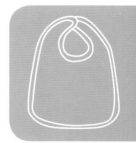

vegetable lasagne

Preheat the oven to 375°F/190°C. Heat the oil in a saucepan, add the onion and garlic, and cook very slowly for about 10 minutes, until soft. Add the zucchini and cook for 2–3 minutes. Add the spinach and stir until just wilted then remove from the heat. Let cool then drain off any liquid.

   Mix the cooked vegetables with the ricotta cheese. If necessary, blanch the lasagne according to the package directions. Cut each lasagna sheet into pieces to fit individual ovenproof dishes about 5 inches/ 12 cm square. Spoon a little tomato sauce into each dish. Layer the lasagne, ricotta cheese mixture, and tomato sauce in each of the dishes. End with a layer of lasagne. Pour cheese sauce over each lasagna and sprinkle with the mozzarella and Parmesan cheeses.

   Bake for about 20–25 minutes, until golden brown.

Prepare: 30 minutes

Cook: 25 minutes

Makes: 3–4 individual lasagne

1 tbsp olive oil

1 red onion, chopped

1 garlic clove, crushed and chopped

3¹/₂ oz/100 g zucchini, sliced

3¹/₂ oz/100 g baby spinach, washed
   and coarsely torn

heaping 1 cup ricotta cheese

3–4 sheets fresh lasagne

1 quantity Tomato or Vegetable
   Sauce

1 quantity Cheese Sauce

3¹/₂ oz/100 g mozzarella cheese,
   coarsely chopped

¹/₂ cup freshly grated Parmesan
   cheese

Children love the sweetness of fruit and it often encourages them to eat meat dishes. Encouraging toddlers to chew meat is sometimes tricky, so you may need to cut the pork into very small dice.

pork & plums with cabbage mash

Prepare: 15 minutes

Cook: 25 minutes

Servings: 1–2

1 large potato, peeled and chopped

2 tsp vegetable oil

½ small onion, thinly sliced

3½ oz/100 g lean pork tenderloin, cut into bite-size pieces

½ tsp chopped fresh sage

2 plums, pitted and sliced

3 tbsp freshly squeezed orange juice

pinch of ground cinnamon

1 tbsp Hoisin sauce or organic ketchup

3–4 tbsp vegetable stock (optional)

½ cup finely shredded savoy cabbage

1–2 tbsp milk (optional)

1 cooked carrot, for serving

Cook the potato in boiling water for about 10 minutes, until tender.

Heat the oil in a small, lidded skillet. Add the onion and cook for about 5 minutes, until golden. Add the pork and cook for 5 minutes, until golden brown on all sides. Add the sage, plums, orange juice, cinnamon, Hoisin sauce, and a little vegetable stock to thin if necessary. Cover and cook gently for 5 minutes, or until the pork is cooked.

Meanwhile, steam or cook the cabbage in a little boiling water for 2–3 minutes, until just tender. Drain and mash the potatoes with a little milk. Stir in the drained cabbage. Serve the pork and cabbage mash with one small, sliced, boiled or steamed carrot.

After a good breakfast and mid-morning drink, some children are not always ready to sit down for lunch. This dish looks like a little snack but is full of good things that will keep up their energy levels until dinnertime.

tex-mex roll-ups

Prepare: 10 minutes

Cook: 30 seconds

Servings: 2

2 corn tortillas

2 tbsp Boston Baked Beans or
   canned organic baked beans,
   mashed

2 tbsp grated cheddar cheese

2–3 tbsp cooked chicken, finely
   chopped or shredded

1 tomato, sliced

1/4 avocado, peeled and cut into
   strips

Put each tortilla on a microwavable plate. Spread the beans over each tortilla and sprinkle with the cheese. Microwave for about 15 seconds, until the cheese melts. Cool slightly. Arrange the chicken, tomato, and avocado on top. Roll up and cut into small pieces.

This recipe makes more chili than you need, but you can freeze it in individual portions for up to one month. You can also serve the chili with rice or on whole wheat toast with cooked baby corn or mild tomato salsa.

baked potato with chili

Prepare: 5 minutes

Cook: 30 minutes–1 hour

Servings: 1 (4–5 servings
for the chili)

1 small baking potato, washed

olive oil, for rubbing

chopped chives, for garnishing

CHILI BEEF

1 tsp olive oil

$^1/_2$ small onion, chopped

4 oz/115 g lean ground beef

$^1/_2$ tsp ground cumin

$^1/_4$ tsp paprika

large pinch of mild chili powder

7 oz/200 g canned chopped
tomatoes in tomato juice

$^1/_2$ tbsp tomato paste

6 tbsp unsalted beef stock

7 oz/200 g canned red kidney beans,
drained and rinsed

Preheat the oven to 400°F/200°C. Rub the potato with olive oil. With a knife, make an incision around the potato about two-thirds of the way up. Place on a baking sheet and cook for 30–60 minutes.

To make the chili, heat the oil in a saucepan and cook the onion for about 5 minutes, until soft. Add the ground beef and brown. Stir in the spices and cook for 1 minute. Add the tomatoes, tomato paste, stock, and beans and simmer for about 30 minutes, until thickened.

Place the potato on a plate. Cut off the top, spoon on a little of the chili beef, and garnish with chives.

Kids love baked beans and sausages but commercial brands of beans are often very high in sugar. However, it's easy to make your own. Make sure you buy pure maple syrup and not the "maple-flavored" variety.

Boston baked beans

Broil the sausages for about 10 minutes, turning frequently during cooking. Put the beans, strained tomatoes, maple syrup, and mustard into a pan. Cook gently for about 10 minutes, until heated through.

Broil the pancetta until crisp and browned. Either chop the sausages and add to the beans in the saucepan or serve the beans, topped with the pancetta, alongside the sausages.

Prepare: 5 minutes

Cook: 15 minutes

Servings: 2

2–4 good-quality small pork
   sausages
14 oz/400 g canned white beans,
   such as cannellini or lima,
   without added salt or sugar,
   drained and rinsed
heaping ¾ cup strained tomatoes
1 tbsp maple syrup
1 tsp whole grain mustard
4 slices thinly sliced pancetta
   or bacon

Make salads interesting by using bright colors and a lot of different textures. Vary the ingredients according to what is available—in the summer cooked, skinned fava beans are delicious and cooked corn and beet add color.

super salad

Prepare: 10 minutes

Servings: 1–2

1 slice day-old ciabatta bread

olive oil, for brushing

few small crisp lettuce leaves

3–4 green beans, cooked
   until just tender, chopped

1 broccoli floret, cooked
   until just tender, chopped

2–3 cherry tomatoes, quartered

1-inch/2.5-cm piece cucumber, diced

¼ small red bell pepper, seeded and
   chopped

2 baby new potatoes, cooked
   and sliced

1 hard-boiled egg, cut into wedges

few shavings of Parmesan cheese

DRESSING

1 tbsp sour cream

1 tbsp olive oil

2 tbsp balsamic vinegar

To make croutons, brush the ciabatta slice on both sides with olive oil and broil on both sides until crisp and golden. Let cool, then cut into chunks.

Tear the lettuce into manageable pieces and arrange in a bowl. Add the beans, chopped broccoli, cherry tomatoes, cucumber, red pepper, potatoes, and egg.

To make a dressing for the salad, mix together the sour cream, olive oil, and balsamic vinegar. Spoon a little of this dressing over the salad and scatter with Parmesan shavings and the croutons.

Desserts are always a treat, but try to make sure your toddler gets to like those that are fruit-based and try to avoid those that are very high in sugar and fat. Always buy plain yogurt and add your own flavors.

baby baked apples with fudge yogurt

Prepare: 15 minutes

Cook: about 15 minutes,
   plus chilling

Servings: 4

heaping ¾ cup whipping cream

heaping ¾ cup plain Greek-style
   yogurt

4 tbsp dark brown sugar

4 small apples

8 plumped dried apricots, chopped

2 tsp butter

To make the fudge yogurt, whip the cream until thick. Fold in the yogurt and put into a bowl. Sprinkle over the brown sugar, then cover and chill in the refrigerator for 1 hour. During chilling, the sugar will liquefy and form a thin layer of "sauce."

Preheat the oven to 400°F/200°C. Wash the apples and remove the cores. Using a sharp knife, make an incision around each apple about halfway up, so the apple can expand during baking. Put the apples in a small ovenproof dish and fill the apples with the apricots. Put a pat of butter on top of each one and bake in the oven for about 15 minutes, or until soft.

Swirl the liquefied sugar through the yogurt and serve with the warm apples.

joining family meals *3 years plus*

By the time children reach their third birthday, the often-difficult toddler behavior starts to pass. Children will now be joining in with most family meals and will, by this stage, have all their teeth, which gives you much more flexibility with the foods you cook. However, the years between the ages of three and five are still very important from a nutritional point of view.

"Breakfast is a very important meal for growing children."

One problem that sometimes arises is when a child of this age really loves milk. Because milk contains calcium it is very important for bone growth. However, it is low in iron and other nutrients that are found in a properly balanced diet. Children who want milk drinks throughout the day will feel full and then not eat their meals. Limit the amount of milk and don't offer it at mealtimes. You can offer lowfat milk if your child is of normal weight and has a varied diet. At the opposite end of the scale, there are some children who don't like drinking milk, but this is easier to deal with, because you just need to increase the amount of cheese, yogurt, or other dairy products they eat to ensure they get sufficient calcium.

During the next couple of years, your child will at some point start nursery and then part- or full-time education. It is, therefore, crucial that your child keeps eating nutritiously—providing healthy food is one of the most important things you can do as a parent. Now that your child is joining family meals, it may be that you have to look at your own diet and make a few healthy but necessary adjustments. One of the best things you can do is to add salt only when it is really necessary in cooking and never have it on the table as a condiment. Salt is found in small amounts in virtually all foods, even in tap water. Try not to buy too many processed foods or prepared meals from the supermarket, because these are often very high in salt. The World Health Organization has set targets of 5 g of salt per day for adults and the following maximum recommended daily amounts for children:

- One to three years old: 2 g salt (800 mg sodium)
- Four to six years old: 3 g salt (1.2 g sodium)
- Seven to ten years old: 5 g salt (2 g sodium)

What can be confusing, when looking at the nutritional label of packaged foods, is that salt is 40% sodium, so 1 g (100 mg) of sodium equals 2.5 g (2,500 mg) of salt. A product that is high in salt is one that contains 0.5 g or more sodium per 100 g, and a product that is low in salt will contain 0.1 g of sodium or less per 100 g. One of the reasons to keep salt and sugar levels to a minimum when children are small is so that they don't get a craving for it but will learn the real flavor of food and reject anything that is too salty.

Breakfast is a very important meal for growing children, and even if you tend to skip it, make sure your child does not. Breakfast helps a child stay full of energy and learn well; it is widely recognized that children who eat breakfast perform better at school. Children often become very interested in sugary cereals and, while these cannot be banned altogether, make sure they are a small part of a variety of breakfasts. Oatmeal, muesli, fruit, and yogurt, smoothies, small muffins, and toasted fruit breads are all quick to prepare.

When a child starts nursery or school, you may need to provide a snack or packed lunch, depending on whether they attend full- or part-time. You don't need to pack much. Most of us tend to put too many things in a lunch box and, if your child is a slow eater or is too interested in talking, you will find most of it is uneaten. It is better to put in a small amount and know that they will have their main family meal when they get home. A couple of tiny sandwiches, a few vegetable sticks, and some small fruit are enough. Don't add potato chips and candy bars because they will eat those and leave the rest.

These make a great start to the day or a filling mid-morning snack. You can make these as tiny muffins or larger ones for older children and adults. Also try using dried cranberries, dates, raisins, or golden raisins.

muesli muffins

Prepare: 15 minutes

Cook: 10–15 minutes for small muffins and 25–30 minutes for larger muffins

Makes: 12 large or 36 small muffins

½ cup plumped dried apricots, chopped

4 tbsp orange juice

2 eggs

⅔ cup sour cream

heaping ⅓ cup sunflower oil

½ cup light brown sugar

2 cups self-rising flour

1 tsp baking powder

TOPPING

heaping ¼ cup light brown sugar

⅔ cup crunchy muesli, lightly crushed

2 tbsp butter, melted

Preheat the oven to 375°F/190°C. Put the apricots and orange juice into a small bowl and let soak for about 15 minutes. Put the eggs into a bowl and beat. Add the sour cream, oil, and sugar. Add the apricot mixture and stir well. Put the flour and baking powder into a bowl and gently stir in the egg and apricot mixture. Do not overmix.

Spoon the batter into paper liners in a muffin pan. Mix together the topping ingredients and sprinkle over the top of the muffins. Bake for about 10–15 minutes for small muffins and 25–30 for larger muffins.

A great treat at any time of day, a delicious fruit smoothie is a good way to tempt young children to eat something first thing in the morning when they are often not interested in breakfast.

smoothies

FRUIT SMOOTHIE

Put all the ingredients into a blender and process until smooth. Pour out and serve with straws.

MALTED BANANA SMOOTHIE

Put all the ingredients into a blender and process until smooth. To make a chocolate variation use chocolate malted milk powder and chocolate ice cream. Pour out and serve with straws.

FRUIT SMOOTHIE

Prepare: 5–10 minutes

Servings: 2

$^1/_2$ mango, peeled and chopped

1 small banana

4–6 strawberries

heaping $^1/_3$ cup Greek-style yogurt, with added honey

$^2/_3$ cup milk

4 ice cubes

MALTED BANANA SMOOTHIE

Prepare: 5 minutes

Servings: 2

1 small banana, chopped

heaping $^3/_4$ cup milk

2 tbsp malted milk powder

4 ice cubes

Once your child starts nursery and, eventually, school, you will need to pack nutritious and enticing lunch boxes. Below are some ideas for sandwich fillings, which can be made and stored for up to 2 days in the refrigerator.

simply super sandwich fillings

CRUNCHY TUNA

Prepare: 10 minutes

7 oz/200 g canned tuna in spring
   water, drained and flaked
1 tbsp canned corn, drained
1 tbsp chopped bell peppers
1 tbsp mayonnaise

FRUITY CHEESE SPREAD

Prepare: 5 minutes

heaping ¹/₃ cup lowfat soft cheese
   or ricotta cheese
1 tbsp chopped pitted dates
2 tbsp chopped plumped dried
   apricots

EGG & BACON

Prepare: 15 minutes

2 hard-boiled eggs, shelled and
   mashed
1 tbsp mayonnaise
2 crisp-cooked slices bacon,
   chopped

HUMMUS

Prepare: 10 minutes, plus time for
   cooking the carrot

heaping ¹/₃ cup hummus
1 small cooked carrot, chopped
1 tbsp chopped cucumber

CHICKEN & AVOCADO

Prepare: 5 minutes

¹/₂ cooked chicken breast, finely
   chopped
¹/₂ small avocado, mashed with
   2 tsp lemon juice

COLESLAW

Prepare: 5 minutes

³/₄ cup coleslaw
1 tbsp coarsely grated cheddar
   cheese
1 thin slice ham, chopped

Mix the ingredients for the fillings together and store in the refrigerator until required.

This salad is good eaten on its own with some crusty bread, but it is also delicious served with room-temperature roast chicken, homecooked ham, or sliced salami. If your toddler likes them, add a few pitted black olives.

warm pasta salad

Prepare: 15 minutes

Cook: 35 minutes

Servings: 4

5 tbsp olive oil

1 tbsp lemon juice

2 garlic cloves, flattened with the
   back of a knife and chopped

1 tsp chopped fresh rosemary

2 tsp chopped fresh thyme

1 red onion, cut into 8 wedges

1 red bell pepper, seeded and
   thickly sliced

1 yellow bell pepper, seeded and
   thickly sliced

4 small zucchini, quartered
   lengthwise

4 plum tomatoes, quartered

9 oz/250 g penne pasta

1 tbsp white wine vinegar

1 tbsp pesto

7 oz/200 g feta cheese, crumbled

handful baby arugula leaves

Preheat the oven to 400°F/200°C. Put 2 tablespoons of oil, the lemon juice, garlic, and herbs into a large baking pan. Add the onion and peppers and toss in the oil mixture. Cook in the oven for 10–15 minutes. Add the zucchini and tomatoes and cook for an additional 10–15 minutes, until the vegetables are soft and lightly charred on the edges.

Meanwhile, cook the pasta according to the package directions. Drain and put into a large bowl. Mix together the remaining oil, the vinegar, and pesto, and pour over the pasta. Add the cooled, cooked vegetables and the cheese and toss gently together. Sprinkle over the arugula and serve warm.

Egg-fried rice is very popular and can be served with many other dishes. It is a great way to get children to eat egg without their realizing it. Young children enjoy the flavors of this Chinese-inspired salmon.

salmon with egg-fried rice

Cut the salmon into 2 pieces and place in a shallow dish. Mix together the honey and soy sauce and brush over the salmon. Let stand for 10 minutes.

Heat 2 teaspoons of the oil and cook the carrot for about 5 minutes. Add the peas and pepper and cook for an additional 5 minutes, until soft. Add the beaten egg and cook over gentle heat, stirring and breaking up the egg into little pieces. Add the cooked rice and heat through for a few minutes.

Heat the remaining oil in a small skillet and cook the salmon for 2–3 minutes on each side. Alternatively, cook the fish under the broiler. Stir the scallion into the rice. Serve the salmon on a bed of spinach and accompanied with the egg-fried rice.

Prepare: 10 minutes

Cook: 20 minutes

Servings: 2

7 oz/200 g skinless salmon fillet

2 tsp honey

1 tbsp light soy sauce

3 tsp vegetable oil

1 small carrot, finely chopped

2 tbsp frozen peas

$^1/_2$ red bell pepper, seeded and
    chopped

1 egg, beaten

heaping $^1/_3$ cup basmati rice, cooked

1 scallion, finely sliced

lightly cooked spinach or bok choy,
    for serving

This makes a great Sunday lunch served with mashed or roast potatoes and some green beans. If there is any left over, it is delicious sliced and eaten cold and even makes a good sandwich filling.

family meatloaf

Prepare: 10 minutes

Cook: 1 hour 5 minutes

Servings: 6

1 lb/450 g lean ground beef

9 oz/250 g ground turkey or chicken

9 oz/250 g good-quality pork
  sausage, removed from the casing

2 slices whole wheat bread, made
  into crumbs

2 eggs, beaten

2 tsp Italian herb seasoning

3 tbsp chopped fresh flat-leaf
  parsley

12 slices bacon or pancetta

1 lb 2 oz/500 g bottled strained
  tomatoes, with added onion

Preheat the oven to 350°F/180°C. Put the ground beef and turkey, sausage, breadcrumbs, beaten egg, and herbs into a bowl and mix well, using your hands.

Line a 9 x 5 x 3-inch/23 x 13 x 8-cm loaf pan with plastic wrap. Put the meat mixture into the pan and press down very well. Invert the pan into a small roasting pan and remove the loaf pan and the plastic wrap. Arrange the bacon slices on top of the meatloaf, cover with foil, and cook in the oven for 1 hour.

Heat the strained tomatoes in a small saucepan. Drain off any excess fat from around the meatloaf. Pour the strained tomatoes into the roasting pan, brushing a little of the sauce over the meatloaf. Return to the oven for 5 minutes. Serve slices of the meatloaf with tomato sauce.

When working with filo dough, keep the unused sheets covered until needed or they will dry out too quickly. You can use leftover cooked chicken or turkey in this recipe—just chop it and add to the sauce.

turkey & broccoli wrap

Prepare: 25 minutes

Cook: 20 minutes

Makes: 4 parcels

3 tbsp vegetable oil

10 oz/280 g turkey or chicken
   breast, cut into thin slivers

6 oz/175 g broccoli, cut into
   tiny florets

½ quantity Cheese Sauce

2 tbsp butter, melted

8 sheets filo dough, each about
   6 x 12 inches/15 x 30 cm

1 tbsp sesame seeds

Preheat the oven to 400°F/200°C. Heat 1 tablespoon of the oil in a skillet and cook the turkey for about 5 minutes, until browned and cooked through. Cool.

Blanch the broccoli florets in boiling water for 30 seconds. Drain and refresh in cold water. Mix the turkey slivers and the Cheese Sauce together and fold in the broccoli. Set aside.

Mix the remaining oil and the melted butter together. Cut the filo sheets in half. Take one sheet and brush sparingly with the oil and butter mixture. Place 3 more pieces on top at angles to each other to form a star shape. Brush a little oil and butter between each sheet. Place one-quarter of the filling in the center, then gather up the dough and pinch together. Brush with a little oil and butter and sprinkle over the sesame seeds. Bake in the oven for 20 minutes, until crisp and golden.

Another family favorite is homemade apple pie. The pie dough is especially light because it is made with self-rising flour. Use other fruits, such as apricots and peaches, and try different fruit combinations.

sugar-frosted fruit pie

Prepare: 25 minutes

Cook: 40 minutes

Servings: 6

2½ cups self-rising flour

¾ cup butter

water, for mixing and brushing

1 tbsp cornstarch

½ cup superfine sugar

1 tsp ground cinnamon

finely grated rind of 1 small orange

finely grated rind of 1 small lemon

8 Granny Smith apples, peeled,
   cored, and sliced

2 tsp lemon juice

cream or ice cream, for serving

TOPPING

1 egg white, beaten until frothy

1 tbsp superfine sugar

Preheat the oven to 400°F/200°C. Place a baking sheet in the oven.

Put the flour into a bowl and rub in the butter until the mixture resembles fine breadcrumbs. Add enough water to mix to a soft but not sticky dough. Roll out just under half the dough on a floured surface and use to line the bottom of a 9-inch/22-cm pie plate.

Mix together the cornstarch, sugar, cinnamon, and orange and lemon rinds and toss together with the apples and lemon juice. Pile the mixture into the dough-lined dish. Dampen the edge of the dough with water. Roll out the remaining dough and use to cover the pie. Roll out any trimmings and cut out leaf shapes. Brush these with water and attach them to the pie. Brush the top of the pie with beaten egg white and sprinkle with sugar. Place the pie on the hot baking sheet in the oven and cook for about 30–40 minutes, until golden brown. Serve with cream or ice cream.

For an occasional sweet treat, you can make these tasty brownies. If you use pieces of broken chocolate, make sure you serve only a small piece of brownie. It also makes a great birthday cake.

double chocolate brownies

Prepare: 20 minutes

Cook: 25 minutes

Servings: 16

5$\frac{1}{2}$ oz/150 g semisweet chocolate
  with a minimum of 70 percent
  cocoa solids

7 tbsp unsalted butter, plus extra
  for greasing

1 tsp vanilla extract

1 cup ground almonds

scant 1 cup superfine sugar

4 eggs, separated

heaping $\frac{1}{2}$ cup chopped raisins
  or pitted dried dates, chopped
  walnuts, or chocolate, broken
  into small pieces

confectioners' sugar, for decorating
  (optional)

Preheat the oven to 350°F/180°C. Grease an 8-inch/20-cm square cake pan and line the bottom.

Put the chocolate and butter in a heatproof bowl, then set the bowl over a saucepan of barely simmering water, making sure that the bottom of the bowl doesn't touch the water, and heat, stirring very occasionally, until melted and smooth.

Carefully remove from the heat and let cool slightly, then stir in the vanilla extract. Add the almonds and superfine sugar, then mix well until combined. Lightly beat the egg yolks in a separate bowl, then stir into the chocolate mixture, with the dried fruit, walnuts, or pieces of chocolate.

Whisk the egg whites in a large, grease-free bowl until stiff peaks form. Gently fold in a large spoonful of the egg whites into the chocolate mixture, then fold in the remainder until well incorporated.

Pour into the prepared pan and bake in the preheated oven for 25 minutes, or until risen and firm on top but moist and gooey in the center. Remove from the oven. Cool in the pan, then turn out.

Remove the lining paper and cut into 16 pieces. Dust with confectioners' sugar to decorate if using.

index

allergies/intolerances 16, 19, 29
apple
  baked, with fudge yogurt 78–79
  and beet dip 43
  chicken, leek and mushroom 36–37
  and pear purée 24, 25
  and plum yogurt 39
  sugar-frosted pie 92–93
apricots 26, 35
avocado 27, 43, 72, 84

babies
  commercial food 29
  homemade food 15
  vegetarian diets 17
  weaning 10, 12–13, 18–19
bacon 84
bananas 27, 83
bean, pea, and zucchini purée 23
beans, boston baked 72, 75
beef 74, 88–89
beet dip 43
bread sticks, with dips 42–3
breakfast 81
broccoli 22, 76, 90–91
brownies, chocolate 94
burgers 55, 67

cabbage mash 70–71
carbohydrates 8, 11
carrots 20, 21, 44
cauliflower, and broccoli purée 22
cheese
  dough sticks 46
  fruity spread 84
  macaroni cheese 36
  sauce 30, 31
  and corn fritters 50
chicken
  and avocado sandwich 84
  leek, mushroom, and apple 36–37
  quesadilla triangles 62
  sweet & sour stir-fry 58–59
  tex-mex roll-ups 72–73
chocolate brownies 94
choking hazards 29, 41
coleslaw 84
cookies, star 64
corn, and cheese fritters 50

dairy products 11, 14, 41, 81
diet 7, 8, 11

dips 42–43, 51
drinks 14, 41, 67, 83

egg and bacon sandwich 84

falafel, with carrot salad 44
fats 8, 53
fiber 9, 53
food intolerances 16
freezing food 15
fruit 11, 51, 54, 78–79, 83, 92–93

hummus 42, 84

ice cream and strawberry sauce 64–65

lamb, with rice and apricots 35
lasagne 69
leek 36–37

macaroni cheese 38
mealtimes 7, 29, 41, 53, 67
measurements 4
meatballs, with spaghetti 45
meatloaf 88–89
melon purée 27
milk 14, 19, 41, 53, 81
minestrone soup 46–47
muesli muffins 82
mushrooms 36–37, 62, 68

nursery school 81, 84
nutrition 8–9, 17, 53, 81

oatmeal 24, 54
omelet, deep pan 56

parsnips, with burgers 55
pasta
  with butternut squash 34
  macaroni cheese 38
  with red pepper sauce 48–49
  salad 86
  spaghetti with meatballs 45
  vegetable lasagna 69
pear, and apple purée 24, 25
peas 23, 58
pizzas 60–61, 67
pork, plums and cabbage mash 70–71
potato
  cabbage mash 70–71
  baked, with chili beef 74

and turnip purée 20, 21
processed foods 67, 81
proteins 9, 11
prune, and apricot purée 26
purées 15, 19–27

quesadilla triangles 62
quinoa, with vegetables 33

raspberries 51
red bell peppers 48–49, 56, 60, 76
rice
  egg-fried 87
  fragrant creamy 63
  infant 15, 19, 20, 21
  with lamb and apricots 35
risotto, spring vegetable 32

salads 44, 76–7, 86
salmon, with egg-fried rice 87
salt 81
sandwich fillings 84–85
sauces 30–31, 48–49, 64
serving size 11, 41
smoothies 83
snacks 41, 53, 67, 81
solid food 12–13, 19, 28–29, 41
soup, minestrone 46–47
spinach, and squash purée 24
squash 24, 32
stir-fry, chicken 58–59
strawberry sauce 64
sugary foods 67

tex-mex roll-ups 72–73
toddlers
  encouraging eating 67, 81
  introducing new foods 53
  nursery school 81, 84
  serving size 11
tomato sauce 30, 60, 69
tuna, sandwich filling 84
turkey parcels, with broccoli 90–91
turnip, and potato purée 20, 21

vegetables 30, 31, 33, 69
vegetarian diets 17
vitamins and minerals 9

yogurt 39, 51, 78–79, 83

zucchini 23, 56, 69